GOD'S

GREATER

LOVE

DANE C. ORTLUND

knowledge, that you may be filled with all the fullness of God." Knowing Christ's love is the means, and being filled with divine fullness is the purpose. We are infused with divine plenitude, fullness, buoyancy, joy, as we experience the love of Christ. We don't go out and attain divine fullness. We receive it. This is the surprise of the Christian life.

This love is the power that burst the created order into existence, and most supremely you, the pinnacle of creation. He created you in order to love you. He knit you together with his hands so that he could pull you into his heart. One day we will stand before him, quietly, unhurriedly, overwhelmed with relief and standing under the felt flood of divine affection in a way we never can here in this life.

Whether you have ignored it, neglected it, squandered it, misunderstood it, or hardened yourself to it—the Lord Jesus Christ approaches you today

Love defines who God is most deeply.

never overestimate it. Who are we—weak, faltering, mixed-motives we—to be filled up with the very fullness of God himself? How can the clay be filled with the fullness of the potter, the plant with the fullness of the gardener, the house with the architect? What breathtaking condescension, what astounding dignifying of us. Yet this is not something God relents to do, wishing he could be doing something else. Filling up his fallen people with his own fullness is what he delights to do. And how does he do this? What is the means by which he fills us with his own fullness? The text tells us: "To know the love of Christ that surpasses

God's love is greater than

even now you conceive.

The Bible says not simply that "God loves" but also that "God is love" (1 John 4:8, 16). Love, for the God of the Bible, is not one activity among others. Love defines who he is most deeply. A love so great and so free that it could not be contained within the uproarious joy of Father, Son, and Spirit but spilled out to create and embrace finite and fallen humans into it. Divine love is inherently spreading, engulfing, embracing, overflowing. He wants you to know a love that is yours even when you feel undeserving or numb. The love of God is not something to see once and believe and then move beyond to other truths or strategies for growing in Christ. The love of God is what we feed on our whole lives long, wading ever more deeply into this endless ocean. And that feeding, that wading, is itself what fosters growth.

Perhaps no passage takes us into the endless love of God for messy sinners as deeply as the end of Ephesians 3. In one of the most spiritually nuclear passages in all the Bible Paul prays to the Father "that according to the riches of his glory he may grant you to be strengthened with power through his Spirit in your inner being, so that Christ may dwell in your hearts through faith—that you, being rooted and grounded in love, may have strength to comprehend with all the saints what is the breadth and length and height and depth, and to know the love of Christ that surpasses knowledge, that you may be filled with all the fullness of God" (Eph. 3:16–19). Here, Paul prays that the Ephesians would be given supernatural power—not power to perform miracles or walk on water or convert their neighbors, but power, such power, the kind that only God himself can give, power to know how much Jesus loves them. Not just to have the love of Christ. To know the love of Christ.

The love of Christ is as expansive as God himself. We can underestimate it. We always do. We can not with arms crossed but with arms open, the very position in which he hung on the cross, and he says to you: None of that matters right now. Don't give it another thought. All that matters now is you and me. You know you are a mess. You are a sinner. Your entire existence has been built around you. Step in out of that storm. Let your heart crack open to Joy. I was punished so that you don't have to be. I was arrested so you could go free. I was indicted so you could be exonerated. I was executed so you could be acquitted. And all of that is just the beginning of my love. That proved my love, but it's not an endpoint; it's only the doorway into my love. Humble yourself enough to receive it. Plunge your parched soul into the sea of my love. There you will find the rest and relief and embrace and friendship your heart longs for.

© 2023 by Dane C. Ortlund. All rights reserved. Printed in China.
Adapted from the book *Deeper* © 2021 by Dane C. Ortlund.
Published by Crossway. Bible references: ESV.

CROSSWAY | **The Lord Jesus saves all who believe in him.**
To learn more about Jesus as Lord and Savior visit ESV.org/Jesus.